NO CAN DO

Books by Julie O'Callaghan

POETRY

Edible Anecdotes (Dolmen Press, 1983)
What's What (Bloodaxe Books, 1991)
No Can Do (Bloodaxe Books, 2000)

CHILDREN'S POETRY

Taking My Pen for a Walk (Orchard Books, 1988)
Two Barks (Bloodaxe Books, 1998)

JULIE O'CALLAGHAN

NO CAN DO

BLOODAXE BOOKS

ISBN: 1 85224 511 5

First published 2000 by
Bloodaxe Books Ltd,
P.O. Box 1SN,
Newcastle upon Tyne NE99 1SN.

Bloodaxe Books Ltd acknowledges
the financial assistance of Northern Arts.

Cover printing by J. Thomson Colour Printers Ltd, Glasgow.

Printed in Great Britain by
Cromwell Press Ltd, Trowbridge, Wiltshire.

for Dennis

Acknowledgements

Acknowledgements are due to the editors of the following publications where some of these poems first appeared: *At the Year's Turning* (Dedalus, 1998), *Cyphers, The Honest Ulsterman, The Irish Times, Poetry Book Society Anthology* (PBS/Hutchinson, 1992), *Poetry Ireland Review, Poetry Now* (Dún Laoghaire / Rathdown, 1998), *Poetry Review, Sibila, The Times Literary Supplement, Time's Tidings* (Anvil, 1999) and *Verse*.

'The Long Room Gallery' was published in a limited edition by Trinity Closet Press in 1994.

Thanks are also due to the Irish Arts Council / An Chomhairle Ealaíon for a bursary.

Contents

PART ONE

after Sei Shonagon

Yukinari Is Glad

When the parcel of square cakes arrived
I wasn't sure how to reply.
Korenaka suggested I just eat them.
But I took a piece of fine red paper
and wrote a one-sentence note,
attached the usual blossoms
and forgot about the whole thing.

Ten minutes later Yukinari
stood outside my room smiling,
telling me how glad he was
I hadn't sent a poem to him.
'I believe women
who are pleased with themselves
churn out endless poetry,' he added.

I bowed, flapped my fan
and looked at him secretly
out of the corner of my eye
to see if he was serious.
Gaze, flutter, flutter.
He got no pleasure from women
who versified at the drop of a hat.

11

The Three-foot Curtain of State

has only the tiniest gap
along the top of its frame.
Luckily that space normally
corresponds to the eye of a man
standing outside the curtain
and the lady inside fanning the air
with her eyelashes.
As long as the couple are
average height and their eyes
speak the same language,
it works perfectly.

Calling Out

a woman's name must be done properly.
During the day a visitor should mumble it
so people won't think he knows
how to pronounce it very well.
But at night that would be wrong.
A gentleman who comes under stars
to visit a lady-in-waiting
must bring a servant with him
who can call out the lady's name.
It's much better to keep the palace
guessing who her admirer might be.

Spring Robe

The most important thing
is to blend the shades of spring
into the layers of your robes.
Forget about brown until autumn.
Concentrate on pink
and you really can't go wrong.
What I feel about patterns
you probably know already:
only the outer robe
should be delicately decorated.
If you can't work out why
I pity you.
It wouldn't take a genius
to see that all your underlayers
are leading up to a magnificent
froth of spectacular peonies
or any other blossom you want.
So long as it takes the breath
from everyone who encounters it.
If it goes unnoticed
it's back to the drawing-board,
try a new dyer.
Life is way too short
for blasé colours.
Look at the peach tree.
Learn from the cherry buds.

Lady Norimitsu

The dog
outside my shutters
once was Lady Norimitsu
in figured silk robes.
When we speak to her,
or if she hears us gossip
behind screens,
she barks and yelps.
Her eyes fill with tears
at an unhappy love story
just the way they did
in her former life.

Pilgrim

Thinking my usual
gloomy thoughts one day
it occurred to me
that I might make some pilgrimages.
'How frightening!'
was my mother's reaction.
She is a very old-fashioned person.
'What about the thugs
on the road to Ishiyama
and the dangerous way
to Mount Kurama –
wouldn't you be scared?'
she asked me
with her head in her hands.
I was allowed
only a short retreat
to Kiyomizu Temple.
But when I arrived
I couldn't sincerely pray.

Reply

I know it's uncouth
to blow my own trumpet,
but when the Chancellor himself

says that I write
snappy replies to notes
I get slightly conceited.

It's not just the words –
I choose a piece of thin
and rare red paper,

use the best ink and brush,
then attach the letter
to a sprig of plum blossom.

Each detail
conveys a special message
of its own.

Yawns

The other ladies
have retired
to their rooms
and the watchmen
are half asleep.
I am artistically arranged
under seven layers
of autumn-shaded robes
and an outer jacket
of damask embroidered
with silk leaves.
I wish I could hear
the wooden clunk
of your servant's clogs
on the pebbles outside my shutters.
If you don't come soon
the rice cakes will have gone stale,
my straw mat may be
stencilled on my face
and my perfectly straight hair
will look like I've
seen a ghost.
The temple bell
has struck three
and my yawns
are as numerous
as the stars.

Conundrums

How can such a stupid insect
as a fly be allowed
to put its clammy feet
on anything it lands on?
But what drives me really crazy
is snow shimmering
on the roof of some pathetic shack.
If a moonbeam strikes it
at the same time
I shake my head
and admit
I'll never understand
the world.

Mosquito's Eyelash

I was trying to have a conversation
with the new Captain of the Inner Palace Guards
but Masamitsu wouldn't go away.

When he asked the Captain
his opinion of paintings on fans,
I whispered wispily, 'Don't answer him.

If we ignore him, maybe he'll go.'
'What's that?' the Captain responded,
'Did you say something?'

Masamitsu, on the other hand, screamed,
'Really! If that's how you talk about me,
I'll stay here all day long.'

It is said of Masamitsu
that he could hear the sound
of a mosquito's eyelash falling.

Time

Only a moment ago
he lay beside me
saying silly poetic things.
The mat is still warm,
incense from his robe
haunts the air.

Bright

We sat on the edge of the veranda
raking ashes to keep warm
and to enjoy the snow
turning pale pink at dusk.

When it was dark
the snow was our lamp.
We talked about snowy subjects
until the dawn bell rang.

Imagine our laughter
and we will thaw out
from a thousand years
to live that way again.

Sutra

It was all perfect:

snow, icicles,
everything frozen
when we went to Hase Temple
on pilgrimage.

In the cell next to ours
a man recited the sutras
hour after hour
in a muffled voice.

I was wishing
he would speak up
but instead he stopped
and blew his nose.

Not in a vulgar way
but in a cultivated style.
What did he pray for
so fervently?

Lady Hyobu

as you all know
is a great friend of mine.
But we don't get on
when it comes to calligraphy.
I was practising my characters
in her room last week
when she said to me,
'Would you mind
not using that brush?'
I never say things like that
if she uses my best brush
or keeps asking
what's inside my writing box
or lets the bristles
soak forever in ink
so they're ruined.
Another thing –
it's very annoying
when I'm sitting there
trying to work on a poem
and she gives me a dirty look
and orders me out of her light.

Sleeves

Call me old-fashioned
but this craze
for wearing uneven sleeves
seems idiotic.
In the first place
they unbalance the robe
so it hangs all lopsided
and the woman wearing them
has to keep tugging
to keep her jacket closed in front.

Evenly matched sleeves
are elegant and graceful
so I don't see why
the fashion gurus
make us wear these ridiculous creations.
Go ahead and wear wide sleeves
(awkward though they are)
during court ceremonies
but let's at least
keep them symmetrical.

Squeamish

Here is a pretty vulgar topic:
rice starch being mixed with water.
You might want to turn the page
because other disgusting things
are those tongs used in fires
during The Festival of the Dead.

There's no use pretending
these items don't exist.
So, whether they are inauspicious or not,
you might as well realise
I'm not squeamish
about mentioning them.

Paper Shortage

Don't make excuses
about how difficult it is
to find a sheet
of delicate red-tinted Chinese paper.

Send a message
on a flat white pebble
or the stem of a hollyhock.
Etch your words
on a purple lotus petal.

White Sound

When rain
whispers
it is snow.

Women with Children Should Keep Them Under Control

I am talking to a woman in my room
who has brought her four-year-old son,
Matsugimi, for an afternoon visit.
The boy is picking up everything
he can reach and poking anything
he's not tall enough to grab.
'Be quiet, Matsugimi,
the grown-ups are speaking,'
his mother whispers indulgently
when he pushes my most precious comb
into her face and demands
to know what it is.
Then he snatches my good fan
and runs after the cat,
waving it at her tail.
'You naughty child,' she smiles,
patting his melon head,
'you mustn't do that, you'll break the fan.'
I anxiously grit my teeth.

A View of Mount Fuji

(for Patrick Scott)

When Emperor Ichijo
asked me what I wanted
as a parting gift
I answered Mount Fuji.

Towards the end
of the Third Month
a Court Chamberlain
led me to new quarters.

I lit a charcoal fire,
arranged my combs and fans
the way I like them
and took in my surroundings.

The lattice was decorated
with patterns of gold leaf
and as I raised the blind
Mount Fuji waited in the distance.

Here I give you Fuji-san
dressed in imperial robes
so that you will not forget me.
He was mine.

Rumble

The seventh month
begins with a moon decoration.
I love to watch
the Royal Party lit up
by fireflies in the heat.
It might sound eccentric
but I wear my willow-green robe
behind the garden lattice
smelling grass smells,
hearing laughter at the pond,
feeling the silk breeze
touch my hair.
An electric summer night:
distant rumble,
lightning on the horizon.

Summer Storm

My cheek rests on a pillow
facing the Iyo blind.
The back of my neck
is hot and sticky
so sleep is impossible.
I wait for the tiniest breeze,
gaze sideways at the lake,
see the summer storm
on the horizon to the east
as I lie on my cot.
The room shakes with thunder,
lightning flashes in the downpour;
rain lashing the Iyo blind
lands like sacred water
from a temple fountain
on me and on my patterned robe.

Auspicious

All day I've been travelling,
trying to avoid an unlucky direction.
Each way is worse than the one before.
To the north-east: ominous clouds,
facing west: a burning fireball.

I am surrounded by inauspicious noises
– screams, barking dogs, sneezes.
When will I learn
to travel the most auspicious road:
toward the quiet garden?

Two Lines

The gentlemen of the Sixth Rank
must be easily pleased.
They have been over-praising
two lines I scribbled
with an old piece of charcoal
late at night.
It was something about
visiting a grass thatched hut
and who would bother
with such a lowly place.
But now I hear
how the Court Nobles
have copied it onto their fans!
His Excellency Tadanobu
even came and pounded
on my half-shutters
looking like the hero
from a romance.
The sleeves from his grape jacket
draped over my screen
are the best reward.

PART TWO

Schmooze-Fest

They bought my life
so I'm off to Lake Geneva, Wisconsin
for a corporate bonding weekend.
I'll get through this schmooze-fest
if it's the last thing I do.
Marv says avoid the loser
in the snappy tie.
He says pack a jumbo bottle
of *Bug-Off*: those little varmints
can be murder.
There goes my watch alarm.
Time for a whacky round
of executive whirlyball.

How the Joint Works

Garbage trucks.
We've got a gizmo
with a robot arm
grabbing the garbage cans
and hoisting them up
so they tilt the refuse
into a disposal unit.
Police in shorts zoom by
on all-terrain-vehicles
chasing villains – cool.
Earth movers push stuff –
sand, mud, gravel.
Cripes, we've got a crew
out there raking up dead fish.
The Park District sends
the sand-sifter tractor
each evening to get rid
of nasty items on the beach.
Traffic Division arranges
big plastic cones
to smooth rush hour flow.
It's like clockwork.
A massive operation.
Bigtime.

Weather

What are ya – slow?
Don't you get it?
Once we sent up those darn astronauts
and all that space garbage
to the outer atmosphere
it wrecked the weather.
For crying out loud
you can't keep puncturing
the sky with those items.
Where do ya think
all the oxygen's going?
It's leaking out the holes, stupid.
Any dummy knows that.
You can hardly breathe anymore.

Home

The Illinois sunrise demonstrates
exactly what an alien you are
in your car on the prairie
heading north to Chicago
where some Irish guy
aimed a hundred years ago.
That's why you're going there
instead of somewhere else.

He is controlling your life
and the direction of your auto.
If he had decided on Boston –
you'd be driving there instead.
Funny how we let this geezer
place us here and give us an accent,
expecting us to live surrounded
by corn and soybean fields.

In a booth at the Dixie Truck Stop
you drink your bottomless coffee
and figure how the rustics to your left
and the military personnel to the rear
were similarly plonked down
in the middle of nowhere.
Simple souls that we are
we now call this region 'Home'.

Outline for Next Chapter

Protagonist decides to try lipstick.
Recalls how co-worker had said,
'You only think you look crummy with lipstick
because you aren't used to it.'
Figures this is true of life in general.
On way to department store
muses on modern civilisation
and mid-season sales in particular.
Examining mark-downs is confronted
with peach linen shirt at a
nevertoberepeated price.
Files merchandise and amount
in the 'current topics' portion
of her psyche.
Saunters to cosmetics counter.
Feels inadequate when asked
'How can I help you be more beautiful?'
by a sales representative
resembling a faded starlet.
Is given many make-up tips
which only a super-model
usually is aware of.
Is completely transformed.
Wistfully remarks,
'If only I'd known how
to look like this years ago!'
Resolves that *Life is a Cabaret*
and that there is no use in sitting
alone in her room.

Biography

Skip the boring bits –
Napoleon, battles,
and whatnot
like that garbage about
politics in old Europe.
Yawnerino.
Page forward to the part
where somebody's illegitimate daughter
gets married to a Duke
against his parents' wishes
and how they spend the rest of their lives
running around different places
trying to find complete perfection.
Stuff you can get your teeth into.

Bagels, Snow

I don't want to
do one of these
'sitting in a bookshop
during January
eating bagels
with my sister
whilst watching
the falling snow
in downtown Chicago
as the lights come on
at dusk' type of deals.
But she is drinking
an oversized cup of cocoa,
there are shelves of reassuring books
beside us, white lights decorate
the winter branches outside
and the tragedy hasn't happened yet
so I need to keep
the snow sparkling,
the cocoa steaming,
the bagels waiting
on a white plate
for as long as possible.

Fire Hydrants

are vital
so you can't park
near them.
They come in handy
for shoe tie-ers,
grandmothers
from the old country
can sit down
and catch their breath.
There are so many
youth programs
in summertime
painting and decorating hydrants
that there must be a lot
of old ladies
with fresh colours
on their flowery backsides.
Cheer the place up
for godsake.
Old Faithful spraying
dusty streets
on a city afternoon –
how can such
a dumb thing as water
change bricks
into a waterfall?
A liquid diamond
sparkles on
your tongue.

Show-off Central

Schnooks are out
cross-country skiing
down Wall Street,
dog-sledding the asphalt
of New York, speed-skating
along 5th Avenue.
I've got my speakers blasting
The Met's *Figaro*.
Dinner will be delivered
from *The Delightful Deli*
during the interval.

Just me and my cozy apartment
suspended mid-air,
mid-town and mid-life
inside a silent blizzard.
The perfect eco-system
for a February Saturday.
You want to see me?
I'm in those aerial shots
of Manhattan – the ones
that make hicks flock here –
skyscrapers with twinkling beacons.

Buildings with thrilling rows
of lit-up windows?
I'm in one
trying not to
gloat.

No Can Do

I know I'm a total party-pooper.
But there's no way
I can go to Red Lobster.
I have to stay home.
I have to rest.
I can't move.

Chip is like:
'How come you don't want
to go out anyplace?'

I'm this huge moose
with no hair,
a cheapo wig and cancer.
And I'm supposed to go
and eat a Seafood Platter?
No can do.

Hog Heaven

First thing in the morning
as I'm scratching my armpit
is to grab a gallon carton
of that Guilt Free Fudge ice cream.
No fat – no sugar:
wouldn't you for godsake?
I said No Fat – No Sugar
you heard right.
During the rest of the time
I chomp on fat-free cookies
dunked in organic soya cream,
pour out fake scrambled eggs
into a non-stick frying pan,
sharpen my fangs on a few healthy
Bavarian low-sodium pretzels.
Sheesh!
I guess I can celebrate
with a wholemeal bran muffin
coated in *I Can't Believe It's Not Butter*
and no-added-sugar fruit spread?

Sipper Lids

It didn't feel so hot
when I found out about
those sipper lids.
We were driving to hardware stores
like it was the good old days.
The air was July
and the sun was too.
'Don't put the brownies
on the dashboard – they'll melt.'
I'm pulling off the lid
on my honey-sweetened coffee,
when my dad tells me not to.
'Watch me' – he picks up his coffee,
puts the lid to his mouth.
(He's doing this and steering.)
As I look over at him
sipping from the little gashes
in the plastic lid,
I know all is lost.
I might as well have been
the older kid from Italy
stuck at the back
of our Chicago classroom
because she didn't speak English.
Some kind of foreigner
who never heard of sipper lids.

Hogging the Chow

I would love to know
who's hogging all the chow
down at that end.
It would interest me greatly.
Do I have to send a
SWAT team over there
to commandeer a few lumps of squash
and a handful of peas?
I seem to recall shelling out
for all this stuff.
Is that the smell of fried chicken in the air
or am I hallucinating
due to lack of nutrition?
My sainted wife
has been turned into stone
with her mouth hanging open
and a bowl of mashed potatoes
hovering three inches off the table.
Let's try banging our plates
with our cutlery.
It works in prison movies.

McDougalmeister's

OK. Time for a chow-down
at McDougalmeister's.
Order me a McChicken Grilled Sandwich,
a McEskimo Double Fudge Sundae,
a McDougalmeister Large Fries.
Oink Oink.
Your ketchup is dripping down
your Disney t-shirt, Mr Slobola.
Lick it off Mickey's ear – feel free.
Are you with me here, people?
This is the pace we're working for:
one-two-three-four-five.
Any dilly-dallys or dawdlers
will get forty lashes
with a wet noodle.
We've got three hundred cornfields
to get through
until we can fill our pie-holes again
at the next McDougalinsky's.

Skinny

All I ever eat is cake.
I eat it at every meal.
Oh and I drink Snapple.
First I take a forkful of cake,
then I wash it down with Mango Cocktail.
That's my secret
on how come
I'm so skinny.

Reflected

in the milky mirror of tea
is my face
looking at the painting
Flatiron Building Reflected
in Car with Figure in Bus.
I can almost see both reflections
at the same time.
That isn't all I can do.
I hear three or four things, too.
A magpie's click, an orchestra,
street drill and keyboard
as I hold the cup to my mouth
looking over the rim
at the Richard Estes painting
and read: 'probably the first picture
I did of reflections + cars'.
Add to that how, as I put down the mug,
I just thought I'd love to write some poems
that feel like these paintings.
Occasionally, everything seems clear,
reflected in everything else.
I won't tell how I had the tea mug
in one hand and a pen in the other,
watching, drinking and writing
at the same time –
you'd think I was showing off.

Not a Nice Place

Holy cow!
You should see that place.
Children have bulletproof backpacks
for their schoolbooks.
People are four feet around.
Men wear skirts,
women power-dress.
All they ever do is complain
about their charcoal-grilled steaks.
It is not a nice place.
War surgeons train in city hospitals
– oi vei, you could get shot
for your Rolex watch
or your Nike boots
or if you look crooked at somebody
on an interstate highway.
Everybody there is weird.
Killer bees go on the rampage.
Lost children are advertised
on milk cartons.
People say 'Have a nice day' to you.
Nuts hide in the woods
with Uzi sub-machine guns.
A grassy hill might be a nuclear silo.
Garbage is pulverised
to the size of a shoe-box.
How can people
live like that?

Short-changed

The gals behind the hosiery counter
have looks of despair on their faces.
Is this any way to leave a cash drawer,
with no quarters or dimes or singles?
How the heck are they supposed to sell
pantyhose without any change?
A customer unfurls a tale
of New Year's Eve hose-horror:
finding a hole near the butterfly
at her ankle when she put them on.
Her entire evening in shreds,
she wore a plain pair.
Hon, look at these snags –
you said you never wore them.
The verdict arrives:
See if there's another pair out.
(Wear them New Year's Eve,
bring them back and get a new pair –
why not?, they mutter.)
And just wait till they get their hands
on the girl who left them no change.

Facing West

Walls of twinkling skyscrapers
need all the help they can get.
They soak up the colours of dusk.

People quit cooking
or stop laughing at the TV
and turn peach, violet and pale blue

– they are facing west.

Autumn Foliage

Have you called the Foliage Hotline
like I asked you to, mister?
We are losing time here, people.
Those trees are getting atmospheric
as we speak.
Listen up, campers, can we have
a little more of the cooperation
and less of the attitude?
We need to place our fannies
in that Cherokee by 10 a.m. – tops.
One lousy gust at this stage
and those gorgeous maple leaves
are rotting debris.

The Long Room Gallery
(Trinity College Dublin)

There is nothing to breathe
here in the Gallery
except old years.
The air from today
goes in one lung
and 1783 comes out the other.
As for spirits,
stand perfectly still
and you will feel them
carousing near your ear.
Tourists down below
think they've seen a ghost
when they spot you
floating through bookcases
over their heads.
On a creaky wooden balcony
you tunnel through centuries,
mountains of books
rising into the cumulus.
You could scale a ladder
up the rockface of knowledge
or search the little white slips
stuck in books
for a personal message
from Swift.
Ancient oxygen,
antique dust particles,
petrified wood...
Who are you kidding?
You belong down there:
baseball caps, chewing gum, videos.

To a Barge Passing on the Horizon

Someone says
there's a law against barges
in January.

Buddy-boy over there
wants to know
what you're loaded with
that couldn't wait for April.

It's obvious to the panel
you are from Indiana
headed for Wisconsin.

Miss Know-all swears she can see
teensy tugs beside your bow
so she figures you must have
an important cargo of SOMETHING.

I see you as an optical illusion
travelling over my father's left shoulder
to barely below his right ear.

Another focuses the telescope on you,
discloses that your name is *Ulysses S. Grant*.

Anyhow, you're moving right along
so, now, even when we stand to one side
and squint out the window
you're history
as a topic around here.

Book Look

What look are you going for?

Let me guess.
I see books and an antique globe.
Am I getting warm?
Colours – OK – I'm seeing bright and dark,
I'm seeing wood and flowers,
I'm seeing hand-woven throws
and wrought-iron chandeliers
where you can attach real candles.
How am I doing?
Are we on the same planet here?
Now it's starting to gel.

I'm visualising a tribal rug,
a wall covered in frames.
Am I headed in the right direction?
So really, what we're talking about
is Ralph Lauren Country House.
You know where they're all in some
moth-eaten mansion in jolly old England
filled with conversation pieces
from like Rangoon or someplace?
Lots of books strewn around.
Books! Oh I just love that Look.

Three-week Residency
(a found poem)

Here is little me
coming to immerse myself
in poetry in a Zen-like room
with wall-length desk
and a window displaying
sub-tropical foliage:
a 'mid-career worker bee
buzzing around that fragrant creature,
our Master Artist'.

My Master instructed me
to write with long lines.
I am like the chameleon
outside my cell
which ope'd its ruby mouth.
I swallow Her advice.
Hark – I will grow
resplendent enough
for a glittering New York publisher.

The Master Artist invites us
to her cottage to discuss Heavy Metal.
She is no stranger to popular music
in general – she danced for 20 minutes
to a Grateful Dead tape.
Know what she is doing?
Pressing the sufficiency of the lyric.
She wants to follow the stutter-step
of tangential discussion.

Our writing grew luxuriant
and expansive, longer-lined.
Master Artist, you effected
a memorable encounter
with artistic Otherness:
you invited painters to a pot-luck supper.
They marched in with Caesar salad,
taco salad, spinach salad, casseroles,
home-made cookies – you name it.

Those painters! They joshed around,
laughed uproariously at unexpected moments,
razzed each other and did not act
like misanthropic Cézannes
or reclusive O'Keeffes at all.
We poets are teetotallers, wholegrainers –
hardly the Rimbaud set.
We slunk off apologetically to bed –
we are early risers.

'There is this matter of the shuttle launch,'
our Master declared one evening.
We would congregate and walk
to a suitably pastoral space to view it.
We all felt the need to observe
such an assertion of earthly might
from the proper perspective.
Who would be the first to convert it
into a *New Yorker* acceptance?

On my last afternoon
I stopped by the Master's cottage.
Despite her tooth problem,
she was perky – I couldn't resist
relating a story about a manatee
I had patted on the head.
I also assured her that my lines now
terminated only when they encountered
the margins of my computer screen.

Trust my Master to see the connection
between the shuttle-launch
and patting the manatee!
A classic piece of metaphysical wit
which looks over its shoulder
at Disney World with visionary 'lift-off'.
Ho-hum, these darn old virtuosos
connecting themselves
to the mind-boggling experience

of being alive.

Writing

I got
real good
grades
in my
poetry workshop.
It was
tough though
revealing my
secret feelings
to a bunch
of people
I didn't know —
but it was
worth it
for a
good grade.

Pelts

Ladies with hair-dos
and shopping bags to die for
pass by with furry friends
clinging desperately to their shoulders.
Mammals' souls hover above their skins
as red nails paw the lingerie reductions
or snake around a coffee cup.
If they could move
they'd give a sharp nip
on the behind to these dames
congregating around cosmetics counters
searching for miracles.
The animals yawn,
listening to the gory details,
noting how perfumed wrists
fumble in bags
for chocolate-covered mints.

Credit Cards

Julie, she says quietly,
why don't you grow up now?
The time is right.
Concentrate as hard as you can
and come out with a hairstyle,
high heels and three children
in a station wagon.
And what about lunch
with your girlfriends?
The Mexican gardener
will be here at three
and you have to bring the kids
to their creative workshops later on.
Have you got that?
Please remember your credit cards, OK?

Things

My guy loves things –
and I'm a shop-till-you-drop gal
so I better get it together.
Here's what one ad says:
'You'll wonder how we got her
into an uncut standard milk bottle –
a unique gift item – Cow in a Bottle, $50.'
Oh man, that would be cool.
But, like, I bet he'd *love*:
'Warsaw Pact Military Binoculars
used by East German border guards
along the Berlin Wall, $499.
Sorry – limit 2 per customer.'
Bummer – which to choose?
He might go ape for a subscription
to *The Potato of the Month Club*...
This is getting totally heavy.
'Cashmere watchcap – built a beefy
two layers thick. Never debilitating.
Lets your head breathe, $105.'
Ouch. Tempting, you'll admit.
What about 'Obsessively hand-crafted sinks,
employed here as waterfalls,
with real water gushing through
them...a kind of existential theatre...
The kicker is that this paradise
is also a kind of prison?' Really.
My dude *has* to have stuff from
Some Like It Hot: Salsa from Hell
or the 12 oz. Ass Kickin' Peanuts.
Capitalism. It blows my mind.
I've mailed my order
for a talisman with his name
in ancient Egyptian hieroglyphics
as a jumping-off point.

Argument with Life

I am arguing with life.
Life says to get tough
play the game.
I am pointing out
that I don't know how
to eat in restaurants alone
or enjoy parties
or love the human race.
I have failings.
Life tries a new angle.
'You're a human, aren't you,
for heaven's sake?
You could meet your friends
for a night out –
what would be so terrible?
Mellow out. Have fun.'
I suggest I can't.
Or won't.
Or don't want to.
I didn't ask to be born,
wisenheimer.

Old Babes

The old babes
feed the pigeons.
They got the circular
about pests on balconies
and chose to ignore it.
Who else is going to drop by
and be glad to see them?
Not their big-shot son.
Or their grandchildren
with buzz-cut hair-dos.
It's pigeons or nothing.

Oh Mom

I

Mom and I are out driving.
We drive up Irish mountains,
we drive down Irish boreens,
we peer over Irish cliffs.
It is almost time
for our coffee break
in a cozy craft emporium.
We could handle a fruit scone
just about now, too, right Mom?
Sometimes you have to stop looking
at those darn stone walls
and those blasted cute little kids
and drink something to remind you
of your home on Sheridan Road –
apartment 22C.

II *Bunratty Folk Park*

Mom and I are at the tourist attractions.
Even when it's raining
and our hair-dos
are one gigantic frizz-ball,
we don't wimp-out.
If the next exhibit
seems to be an authentic
fisherman's cottage (rocks hanging
on the thatch so the roof won't blow off)
we go with the flow
and take a few snapshots.
Say there are fifty 11-year-olds
eating their packed lunches
in the steamy tea-shop, does it bug us?
No way – it's a happening.
Outside, every shape puddle
you could ever dream of!

Hey Mom, it's time to go down
to the genuine old-time Irish village
so hold up that umbrella,
keep your camera handy
and prepare to stroll
right back into the past.

III *Jury's Cabaret*

We even almost get
a tear in our eye
when the guy in the leprechaun suit
sings 'Danny Boy'.

IV *Grub*

Mom and I would like to say
that the chow just wasn't *us*.
How many french fries
can one person eat
before their plumbing clogs?
But, we will admit
it was an interesting experience
and it reminded us of
those animal-fat-ridden
days of yore.

V *Blarney at Killarney*

I think I can speak for us both
when I say we wouldn't have minded
if somebody could've killed the rain.
It wouldn't have bothered us
in the least if the sun had come out.
So Mom and I decided
to take a tour boat – *The Lily of Killarney* –
to shelter from the dampness.
No dice.
Too windy on the lakes.

We checked into a hotel
and looked down at tubercular horses
waiting to haul tourists through town.
We gave ourselves a pep-talk:
'This is ancient Irish rain –
the real McCoy – get into it!'
Then we found the tastiest
lobster soup in the North Atlantic
to heat our guts.
A luxurious bath, a little TV:
Mom and I were new gals.

PART THREE

in memory of my father,
Jack O'Callaghan

Alla Luna
a lunar cycle

Last summer
we lived
on the planet
of purest sadness
looking at people
in the streets
like aliens –
looking at each day
as if it were the last.
We spoke to the moon
without words,
without hope.

*

There was a blue pool
in the sky.
We liked swimming
up there when the moon
and some stars
floated in the water.
You had to be careful
not to butterfly
through a cloud
or dog paddle
into the universe.

*

What was the deal last summer?
We were surrounded
by sky in all directions.
If it wasn't dawn over the lake
it was dusk over the buildings.

Not to mention lightning,
orbiting sky furniture
like stars, planets,
then examining the moon
through your telescope.
All we ever did
was try to sit still
holding our breath
watching the heavens
for a sign.

*

Oh really –
let's all gaze at the moon
and have a nervous breakdown
since life stinks.
I was looking at the lake sideways,
my head on a pillow
wishing and wishing
you would get better.
The moon went blurry:
space-garbage sneering
at me and my sadness.

*

A year ago
I stood at the window
high in the sky crying.
I focussed my father's telescope,
saw lunar mountains, craters, valleys.
'Well, moon,' I said,
'How can I ever be happy again
when my father is disappearing
to a place I can't visualise?'
Luna, I watched you change
all summer into a harvest moon
just before he died.

*

If you were still
in this solar system
we'd be e-mailing
comet sightings
to each other like crazy
and you'd have flipped
watching Hale-Bopp
through your skyscraper windows
on Sheridan Road.
But now I guess
you're some kind of asteroid yourself
travelling to wherever.
Great timing, Jack.
You're missing everything.

The Deal

It cost everything
but he bought a year.
And once it was his
he owned the sky,
a couple of volcanoes
and every molecule
in the universe.
He figured it was pricey
but hey – it was all his.
Minutes and quarter hours
were his as far
as the eye could see.
As for months, twelve big ones
all in a row.
By the time his
daily desk diary
was down to two pages
he had hammered out
a rock-solid deal
on what was to follow.

Touring the Museum of You

Our first display
is the Little Orphan Annie stamp
discovered beside his bed
where the dog is saying ARF
in a bubble over its head.
Then we come to the brightly knitted hat
used in a long winter of chemotherapy.
Several microscopic skin cells
are embedded in the wool.
The last known photograph he took
is of an old Illinois barn
outside Galena in July 1996.
Please don't lean on the glass.
Domestic archaeology
has unearthed a perfect crescent
toenail clipping.
Here we have a gallon of teardrops
lovingly bottled.
This used tube of bronzer
was how he masked
the harsh truth from the world.

Feel free to roam around.

Over

When he saw geese
gathering on a lake in Wisconsin
he said, 'Oh no – summer's almost over.'

Over? It was still hot.
Summer thunderstorms still pounded
nightly on the roof.

Pleeeeeeeeease

Oh for god's sake –
can't we forget it
and you come back to life
and I still travel home
and visit eateries with you in Chicago
and you still blab on about boats and bikes
and we both get on each other's nerves
and you make some pancakes
and then we listen to *Prairie Home Companion*
and after that a bunch of people arrive
and that annoys me
and you ask me funny questions
and we look at articles and the Internet
and you blab on about health
and we get on each other's nerves
and I say let's go down to the beach
and we rent a kooky video
and we make popcorn
and talk on the phone
to all the family – OK?

Sketches for an Elegy

Jack and I are resting
under a weeping willow
beside the beach
I want to stop
asking silly questions
and talk about
important topics
such as
which colour he likes best

*   *   *

it could ruin
a person's outlook
on a jaunty
August morning
to wake up and hear
the Death March on WFMT
and then see
your ghostly bald father
facing the music
at the table
attempting to eat
a bowl of Cheerios

*   *   *

staring from his bed,
he asked, 'How long
did that doctor say?
Was it nine to ten months?
Or was it eight to twelve?'
when I told him six to eight
he shook his head
'Just look at that sky'

*   *   *

a cold start to the summer –
everything was haywire
mist all over the skyscrapers
and no customers
down at the beach

*   *   *

we stood in the park
looking for exotic migrating birds
resting on their way north
for the summer
yellow and blue and red birds
everywhere

*   *   *

sitting around
the chemotherapy room
for hours
I read all the magazines – twice
listening to the others
talk about the price of wigs
the great plumber
they had found

*   *   *

Sunday in August
nothing much doing
we go and get groceries
you need a bench to rest on
so we head for the beach
between the skyscrapers
once you feel better
we take off our shoes
and wade in the lake

*   *   *

a lunatic in the bank
telling the cashier
her life story
– poor bugger
you say

*   *   *

you pull me over and whisper
'See this guy. I've known him for years
– watch what happens when we pass by'
nothing
'Nobody recognises me anymore'

*   *   *

he hears me arranging the flight
'Can't you stay another week?'
how was I supposed to know
he'd have only
three more of his own?

*   *   *

we let you go alone
to pick up
your camera lens downtown
but I worried
the whole time
what if you lost your balance
what if you couldn't walk any further

*   *   *

we're watching David Letterman
and you're paging through
the L.L. Bean summer sale catalogue
you see a shirt you like
and say, 'I won't need it
but one of the boys
could have it'

    *   *   *

you lean forward
and I see a big
pillowy thing
protruding from your side
'It's my liver'

    *   *   *

you have hand spasms
and you can't eat
you can't walk very far
you have no hair
but you can see the sky
the lake
the sunset to the west
so you're OK

    *   *   *

you scratched your name
into cameras, pens, Swiss Army Knives
you etched your name
into sidewalks, kites, clouds, days

    *   *   *

the monk eating pasta
in Dubuque Iowa
was the one I needed
to tell me something helpful
or at least not scary
– no use: he didn't have secrets
of the universe
just a plate of vermicelli

*   *   *

we were running
around the park
and down to the beach
picking up trash
the slobs
had left behind
hey slobs: no one's left
to pick up your garbage
why not go nuts

*   *   *

some were shocked
some looked away
others didn't recognise you
some got all teary
a few opted for chirpy
the doorman slapped your back
and said you looked great
on the bus
people stood up
to let you sit down

*   *   *

the last entire day
I will ever see you
is Chicago Air Show day
– for godsake
it isn't that often
you're having brunch
on the 22nd floor
and a Stealth Bomber
flies past the window
like a black triangle
from the planet Death

*　*　*

in that story
you're three or four
hanging out in the 1930s
in your Irish grandfather's room
he's sick and depressed
but you want him
to play with you:
you toss the rubber ball
in his direction
– as you're telling me
your voice changes
weeping, you say
'All I wanted
was for him to toss it back –
he wouldn't do it'

*　*　*

when someone
can hardly walk
hardly breathe
hardly move
and needs to rest
on a fire hydrant
beside rush hour traffic
you start to panic
trying to figure out
how you'll get him home
a few more blocks

*   *   *

the merchandise you ordered
arrived after you had died
we wondered
what it was
you felt you needed
in your last days
we tore it open
like a secret message
that would explain everything
you wanted us to know:
a tall white chef's hat

*   *   *

you tried to scribble
directions down for us nudniks:
taxes, good repairmen,
what to do
if the pipes froze,
how to apply
for a property assessment
pages and pages
on how to live

*   *   *

I wanted to belt
every person
who grabbed your arm
and put on a pitying voice
I wanted to guard you
from anyone shaking their head
dabbing their eyes
they could save their pity
for somebody else

*   *   *

sitting in the children's section
on a little chair
wearing your HANGTIME baseball cap
you page through a silly book
and nearly forget

*   *   *

there isn't much hope
80% are dead
within 16 months
but he'll try a few things
and see how it goes

*   *   *

driving you to chemotherapy
I realised I couldn't depend
on you anymore
my strong father

*   *   *

Miss You-Know-Who
wore skeleton earrings
with light-up red eyes
beneath a black cowboy hat
complementing her silver metallic
baseball jacket and knit mini-skirt
to your Memorial Service
– you would have been proud
of her genius at being insane

        *   *   *

my meals boiled down
to microwave bowls and minutes
you would holler
from the bedroom
three minutes for peas
or seven for a potato
five minutes for fish
it didn't matter
gourmet wasn't called for
everything tasted like dirt

        *   *   *

you still laughed at *Seinfeld*
and watered your plants
and read *The New Yorker*
and the Tuesday Science section
OK, it hurt a lot
and you said you'd never wear
your bike helmet again
but dying was easier
than I'd thought

        *   *   *

when we were pretending you were OK
we planned a trip up the Missouri
like Lewis & Clark
what boat what route what time-frame
we studied *Undaunted Courage* for pointers
it would be great

    *   *   *

this is a foreign year to you
things will become unfamiliar
inventions you never heard of
gadgets you never used
you loved new developments

    *   *   *

after everything
poison
scars
laser beams of radiation
he says the tumours
are bigger than ever
there is just one more thing
he can try
you asked how it would be
dying – talk me through it
then started painting a picture
of the red barn we saw near the Mississippi

    *   *   *

printing up checks
paying those bills
licking stamps
making calls
searching catalogues
filling in forms
finding things out

     *   *   *

early on
when you still had some energy
we went for a spring walk
in Lincoln Park
and saw a man making a reed sculpture
floating on a pond
you wanted to know
how they float
where did he get the reed
would it eventually sink
who commissioned it
what made him want to
create environmental sculpture
you needed to know

     *   *   *

at the monastery
we each got a room
to think in
you did your thinking
asleep

     *   *   *

you didn't want to take the white stuff
but I made you do it twice a day
you complained
but you still drank it
how could you live without eating
that's what the white stuff did
it made hunger

*   *   *

Jack and me
on fold-up chairs
at the funeral parlour
my cousin's in that coffin
beside the flowers
relatives bending over
to talk to you
eyes everywhere noting
your ghostly appearance

*   *   *

would you do me
just one favour?
quit sitting like that
quit staring at the sky
don't sit and stare
you aren't the sit-and-stare type
go fix something
get out your tools
get busy and hammer

*   *   *

I'm blabbing away
about Irish people
you don't know
or houses
you'll never see
forgive me
it's just my way
of being inconsolable

＊　＊　＊

remember how you told me
your mom used to
stroke your forehead and say,
'there, there' and how that
always made you feel better

＊　＊　＊

what do I need to say about you
I didn't say before
you let me keep a horse in the city
– now that was nuts right there
you took me on a fossil-hunting expedition
and gave me Navajo earrings

＊　＊　＊

when he was crying
he said, 'I'm not sad –
just sentimental'

＊　＊　＊

the last page
about that summer
must be on the topic
of beaches
and how you loved them
and the machines which cleaned them
the police patrolling them
little old Russian ladies on the benches
the whackos dancing around on them
in the middle of the night
the boats floating on them
barges on the horizon
and the pier we walked down
to scatter your ashes